Don't Bug Me; I'm Quilling!

Paper Quilling Projects

Dana Woodard

All of the step-by-step photographs in this publication were taken by and feature the author, Dana Woodard, demonstrating how to create each project. No other models were used.

Front cover: background paper used from the Susan Winget Nature Designer Paper collection by K&Company
www.kandcompany.com

DEDICATION

This book is dedicated to my mother, Brenda Jorgensen, who has always been my rock, always encouraged me to do the best I can, and to follow my dreams. She was the first to introduce me to the craft of quilling and she is the first person I always show my newest designs to. She shares the love of crafts and nature that I do and has taught me so much.

Love you mom!

CONTENTS

Filigree Butterfly

Level - Easy

The directions for this butterfly design indicate pinks and blues as the colours to be used. However, you may choose which ever colours you wish. The butterfly looks stunning in what ever colours you may choose.

You Will Need:

- 1 quilling comb tool (or hair comb)
- 1 strip of black 1/8" (3 mm) quilling paper, 6 inches (15.5 cm) long
- 2 strips of black 1/8" (3 mm) quilling paper, 2 1/4 inches (6 cm) long
- 1 strip of black 1/8" (3 mm) quilling paper, 2 inches (5 cm) long
- 2 strips of dark pink 1/8" (3 mm) quilling paper, 4 inches (10.5 cm) long
- 2 strips of dark pink 1/8" (3 mm) quilling paper, 4 ½ inches (11.5 cm) long
- 2 strips of light pink 1/8" (3 mm) quilling paper, 2 1/4 inch (6 cm) long
- 2 strip of light pink 1/8" (3 mm) quilling paper, 1 ½ inches (4 cm) long
- 4 strip of light pink 1/8" (3 mm) quilling paper, 2 inches (5 cm) long
- 2 strip of light pink 1/8" (3 mm) quilling paper, 3 inches (7.5 cm) long
- 2 strip of light pink 1/8" (3 mm) quilling paper, 3 ½ inches (9 cm) long
- 2 strip of light blue 1/8" (3 mm) quilling paper, 2 inches (5 cm) long
- 2 strip of light blue 1/8" (3 mm) quilling paper, 1 3/4 inches (4.5 cm) long
- 2 strip of light blue 1/8" (3 mm) quilling paper, 2 1/4 inches (6 cm) long

Making The Body:

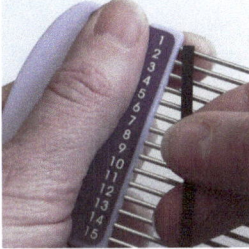

1. With the 6 inch strip of black, begin to wrap it around the first prong of the quilling comb.

2. Wrap the black strip all the way down to the eighth prong.

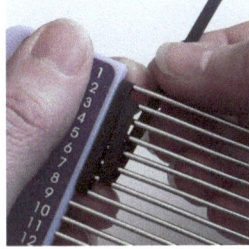

3. Wrap back up to prong two and then back down again to prong 7.

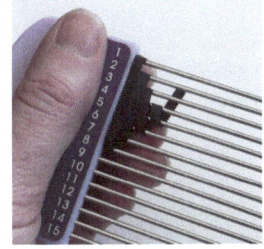

4. Continue to wrap up and down, alternating between the high and low numbers until you reach the center.

5. Slide the wrapped strip off of the prongs.

6. Glue both of the ends in place so that it will not unravel.

**Note: If you do not have a quilling comb, try using a hair comb. Or, just make a loose coil and pinch both ends to a point.

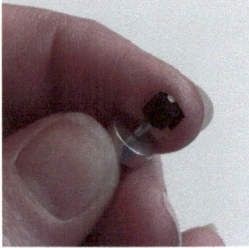

1. Take one of the 2 ¼ inch black strips and roll it into a tight coil.

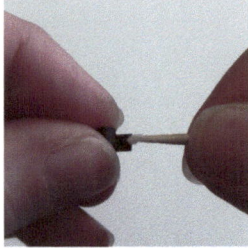

2. Glue the end so that it does not unravel. This is an eye.

3. Repeat with the other 2 ¼ inch black strip for the second eye. Glue the two eyes together.

4. Glue the eyes onto the tip of one end of the body.

5. Take the 2 inch black strip and fold it in half.

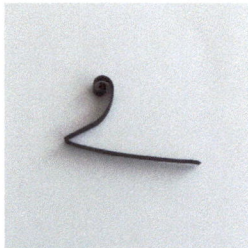

6. Coil one end of the strip outwards about half way down to the fold.

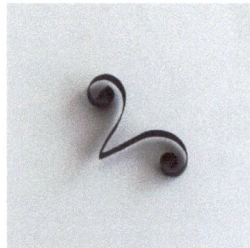

7. Coil the other end of the strip going in the opposite direction. These are the antennae.

8. Glue the antennae to the top of the head in between the two eyes.

Making The Top Wings:

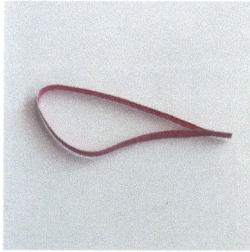

1. Take one of the 4 inch dark pink strips and form it into the shape shown above, glueing the ends together about a ¼ inch at the end.

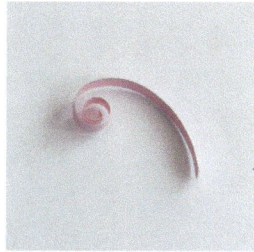

2. Take one of the 2 ¼ inch light pink strips and make a loose coil at one end leaving about an inch of a slightly curved tail.

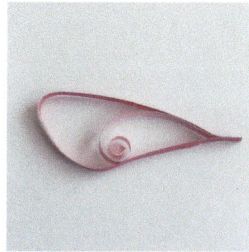

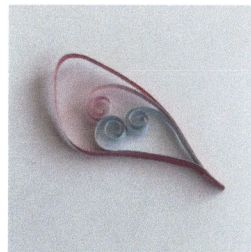

3. Glue this to the top of the inside of the dark pink shape that you have just created. Make sure that the tail end fits snug into the pointed end of the dark pink shape.

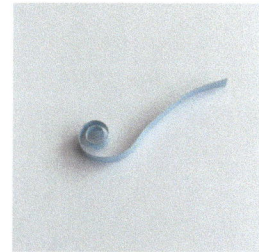

4. Take one of the 2 inch light blue strips and make a loose coil at one end leaving about ¾ inch of a slightly curved tail.

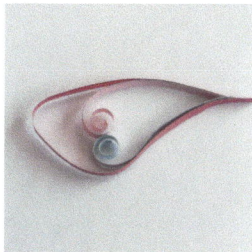

5. Glue this light blue coil to the top of the inside of the dark pink shape just under the light pink coil that you just glued on.

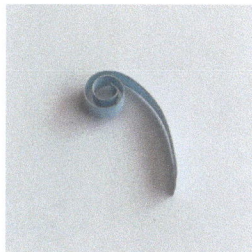

6. Take one of the 1 ¾ inch light blue strips and make a loose coil at one end leaving about an inch of a slightly curved tail.

7. Glue this coil to the inside bottom of the dark pink shape. Face the coil in the opposite direction of the first two so that you have almost a heart shape.

8. Take one of the 1 ½ inch light pink strips and make a loose coil at one end leaving about an inch of a slightly curved tail.

9

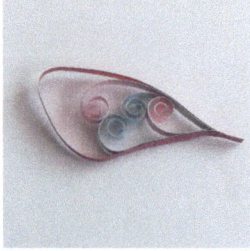

9. Glue the pink coil to the inside bottom of the dark pink shape just below the blue one.

10. Take one of the 2 ½ inch dark pink strips and make a tight coil.

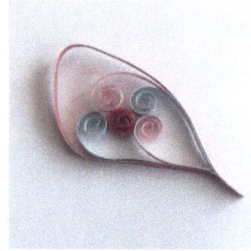

11. Arrange the dark pink coil so that it is touching the tops of all of the other coils and glue it in place.

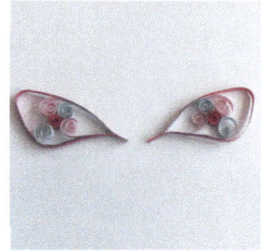

12. Repeat steps 1 to 11 to make the second top wing. Try to get the two wings to look as much alike as possible.

Making The Bottom Wings:

1. Take the 4 ½ inch dark pink strip and make a loose coil at one end, leaving about 2 inches of a pronounced curved tail. It will be in almost a "C" shape.

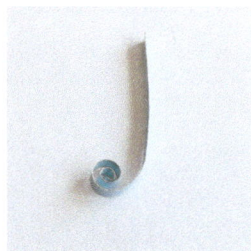

2. Take one of the 2 ¼ inch light blue strips and create a loose coil at one end leaving about a 1 ¼ inch tail. The tail of the coil should stay fairly straight.

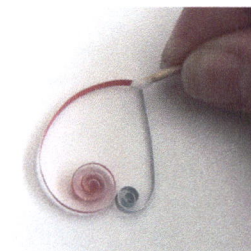

3. Glue the two tails together at almost right angles to each other. Also glue the ends where the two coils meet.

4. Take the 3 ½ inch light pink strip and roll it into a coil (about ¼ inch in diameter) and glue the end so that it doesn't unravel.

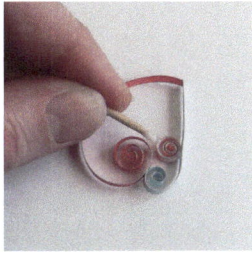

5. Glue the light pink coil in between the dark pink coil and the light blue coil about a ½ inch down from the tail of the light blue coil.

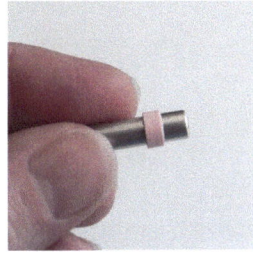

6. Take the 3 inch light pink strip and roll it into a circle about ¼ inch in diameter. It is easiest to do this by wrapping the strip around your quilling tool or a small pencil. Glue the end so that it doesn't unravel.

7. Glue the circle between the coiled end and the curved end of the dark pink coil. Set this part of the bottom wing aside for now.

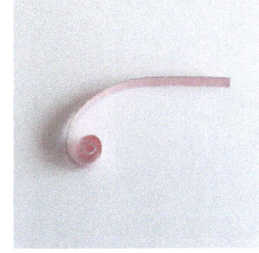

8. Take one of the 2 inch light pink strips and make a loose coil at one end leaving about a 1 ¼ inch of a tail that curves in the same direction as the dark pink coil you just made in step 1.

9. Take one of the 1 ¾ inch light blue strips and make a loose coil at one end leaving about a ¾ inch tail that curves in the opposite direction as the light pink coil you just made.

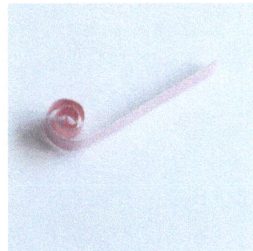

10. Take one of the 2 inch light pink strips and make a loose coil at one end leaving about 1 inch of a tail that curves in the same direction as the light blue coil you just made.

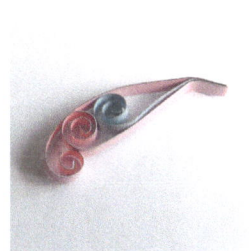

11. Take all three coils you have just made and glue the tail ends together about ¼ inch long. Once glued, fold the tail ends on a slight angle at the ¼ inch mark.

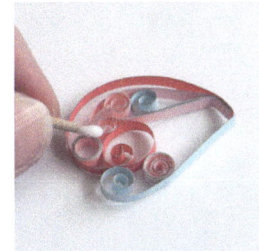

12. Glue the coils from step 11 to the inside top of the dark pink coil. Also glue the top of the longest light pink coil to the top of the dark pink coil.

Putting the Butterfly Together:

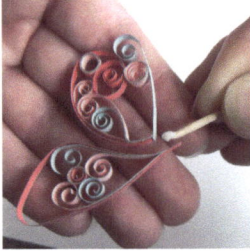

1. Take one of the top wings and one of the bottom wings and glue them together along the flat edges.

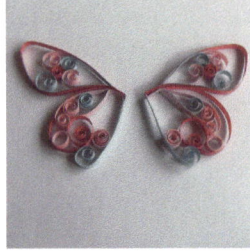

2. Repeat for the other top and bottom wings.

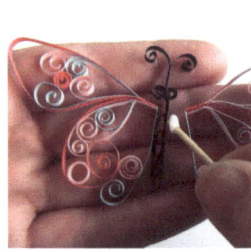

3. Glue the wings onto each side of the body.

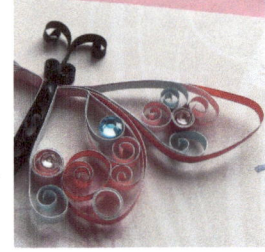

4. Your filigree butterfly is complete. If you would like, you can add glitter, rhinestones, or some metalic inks from a rubber stamp pad for added glamour.

Butterfly Of Circles

Level – Easy

- 1 strip of red 1/8" (3 mm) quilling paper, 6 ½ inches (16.5 cm) long
- 2 strips of red 1/8" (3 mm) quilling paper, 2 ½ inches (6.5 cm) long
- 3 strips of red 1/8" (3 mm) quilling paper, 2 inches (5 cm) long
- 4 strips of red 1/8" (3 mm) quilling paper, 4 inch (10 cm) long
- 2 strips of red 1/8" (3 mm) quilling paper, 2 ¼ inches (5.5 cm) long
- 10 strips of red 1/8" (3 mm) quilling paper, 7 inches (17.5 cm) long
- 14 strips of red 1/8" (3 mm) quilling paper, 1 ½ inches (3.5 cm) long
- 2 strips of red 1/8" (3 mm) quilling paper, 2 ½ inches (6.5 cm) long

Making The Body:

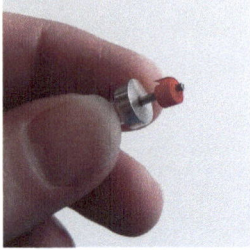

1. Take the 6 ½ inch red strip and roll it into a loose coil.

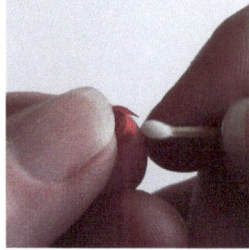

2. Glue the end of the red coil so that it does not unravel.

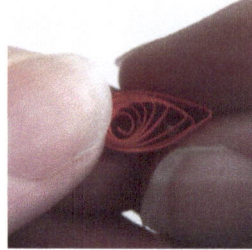

3. Pinch one end of the coil so that it is now in a tear drop shape.

4. Take one of the 2 ½ inch red strips and roll it into a loose coil.

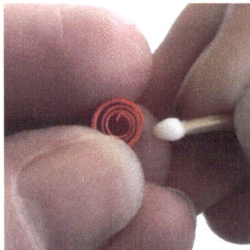

5. Glue the end of the coil so that it does not unravel.

6. Glue the rolled coil to the rounded end of the tear drop shape.

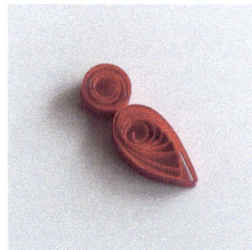

7. Set this aside for a moment while you work on making the head.

1. *Take one of the 2 ½ inch red strips and roll it into a loose coil, making sure to glue the end so that it does not unravel. This is the head.*

2. *Take the 2 inch red strip and roll one end of it about ¼ inch*

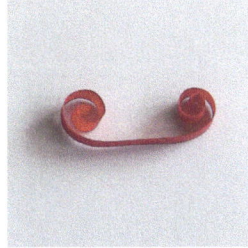

3. *Roll the other end in the same direction about ¼ inch.*

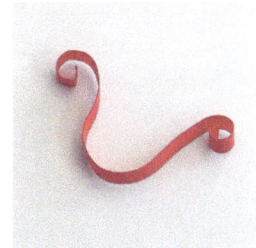

4. *Curve the two rolled ends towards each other so that they make a fancy "U" shape. These are the antennae.*

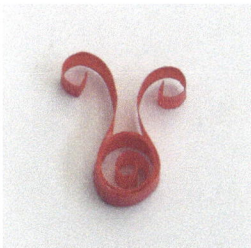

5. *Take the head and glue it into the valley of the antennae's "U" shape.*

6. *Glue the head and antennae to the rest of the body.*

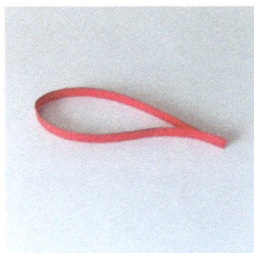

1. Take one of the 4 inch red strips and form it into a large tear drop shape, gluing the ends together about ¼ inch.

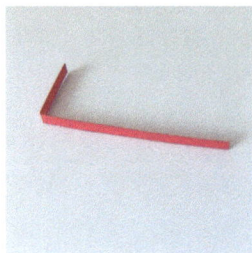

2. Take one of the 2 ¼ inch red strips and make a fold in it about ½ inch up one end.

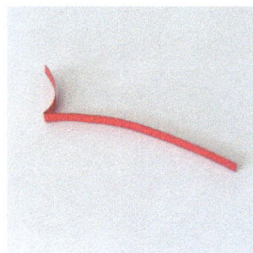

3. Curve the shorter end of the fold up slightly.

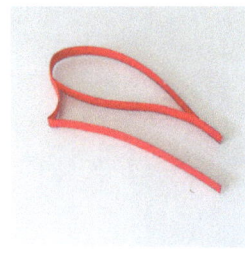

4. Glue one end of the curved folded end to one side of the rounded end of the tear drop shape.

5. Take one of the 2 inch red strips and make a fold about 1/8 inch from one end.

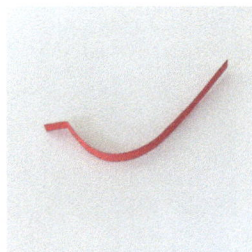

6. Just past the fold, make a curve in the bottom section so that it looks like half of a tear drop.

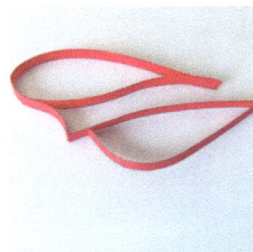

7. Glue the small fold of this strip about 1/8 inch away from the fold line of the other strip you made in step 2.

8. Also glue the two tail ends of the folded pieces together. Then set this aside for a few moments.

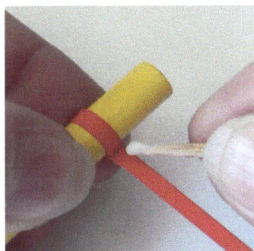

9. Take one of the 7 inch red strips and wind it around a round pencil. Be sure to glue the end before you begin so that it does not unravel.

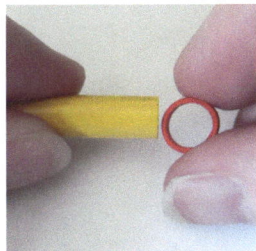

10. Once the entire strip has been wound around the pencil, glue the end in place and then slide the newly formed circle off of the pencil.

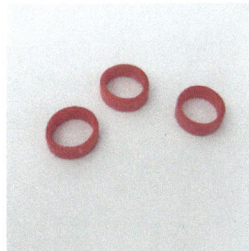

11. Repeat steps 9 and 10 for two more of the 7 inch strips until you have 3 circles made.

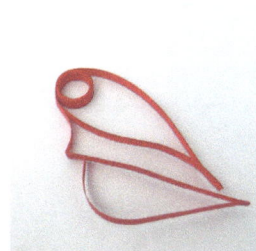

12. Take one of the circles you have just made and glue it to the top, inside of the teardrop shape of the wing.

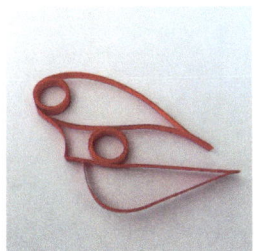

13. Take the second circle and glue it between the two horizontal lines in the wing (It should sit more to the right of the circle above it. About ¼ " from the left edge.)

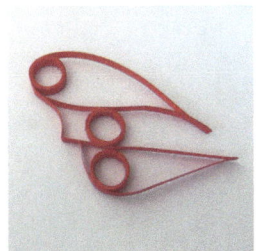

14. Take the third circle and glue it to the bottom inside curve of the wing.

15. Take one of the 1 ½ inch red strips and roll it into a loose coil and glue the end so that it doesn't unravel.

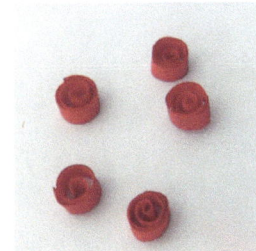

16. Repeat step 15 with 4 more of the 1 ½ " strips so that you have 5 loose coils all together.

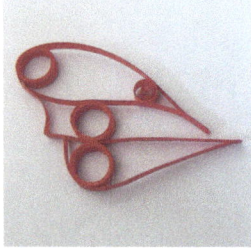

17. *Take one of the loose coils and glue it to the inner side of the teardrop shape where it comes to a point.*

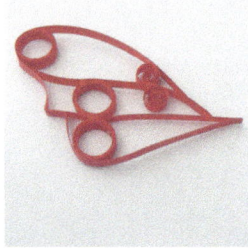

18. *Take the second loose coil and glue it underneath the first coil.*

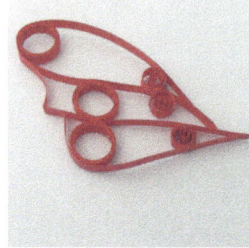

19. *Take the third loose coil and glue it to the inner point on the bottom part of the wing.*

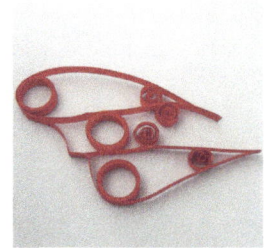

20. *Take the fourth loose coil and glue it to the right of the middle open circle on the wing.*

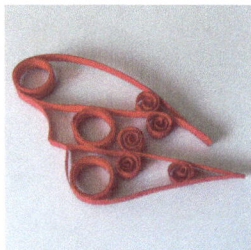

21. *Glue the fifth coil directly below , and slightly to the left of the fourth coil.*

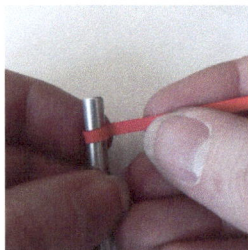

22. *Take a strip of 2 ½ " red paper and wrap it around a pencil or the end of your quilling tool (one that is smaller in width than the pencil you used previously).*

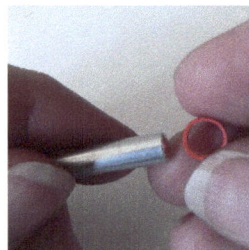

23. *Glue the end so that it does not unravel and then slide it off the pencil or quilling tool.*

24. *You now have an open circle that is about ¼ " in diameter.*

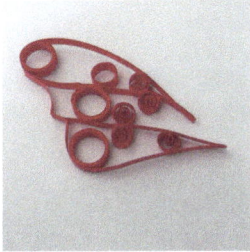

25. Glue the open circle directly above and slightly to the right of the larger middle circle.

26. Repeat steps 1 to 25 to create a second wing.

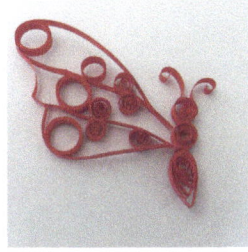

27. Glue one wing to the middle section of the body.

28. Glue the second wing to the other side of the body.

Making The Bottom Wings:

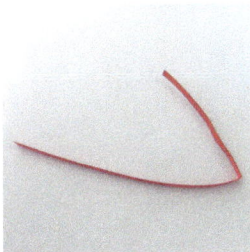

1. Take one of the 4 inch strips and fold it about 1 ¾ " from one end.

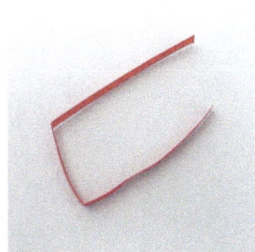

2. Make a second fold in the same direction about 1 inch past the first fold.

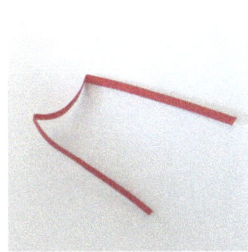

3. Make a curve in between the two folds so that it looks something like an "M" shape.

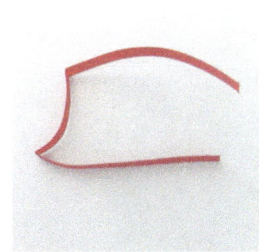

4. Make a slight curve on one of the long ends of the "M".

5. *Glue the curved tail end underneath the bottom of one of the top wings so that it is resting up against the body.*

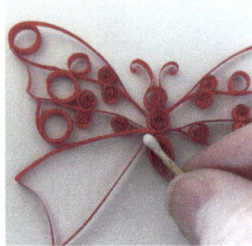

6. *Glue the other tail end to the body.*

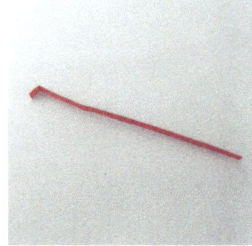

7. *Take one of the 2 ¼ " strips and make a fold at one end about 1/8 of an inch down.*

8. *Make a second fold in the same direction about ¾ of an inch past the first one.*

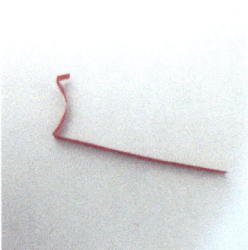

9. *Make a curve in between the two folds.*

10. *Glue the shortest fold under the tip of the bottom wing.*

11. *Glue the longest tail end to the middle of the body.*

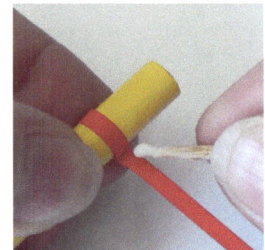

12. *Take one of the 7 inch red strips and wind it around a round pencil. Be sure to glue the end before you begin so that it does not unravel.*

20

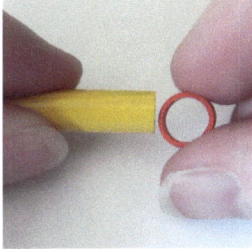

13. Once the entire strip has been wound around the pencil, glue the end in place and then slide the newly formed circle off of the pencil.

14. Repeat steps 12 and 13 to make a second circle.

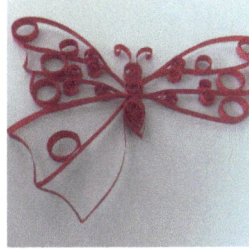

15. Glue one of the circles in the middle of the top part of the inside bottom wing of the butterfly.

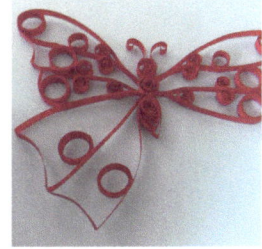

16. Glue the second circle to the inside bottom middle of the bottom wing.

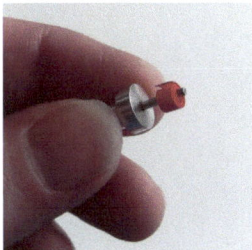

17. Take one of the 1 ½ inch red strips and roll it into a loose coil.

18. Glue the end so that it doesn't unravel.

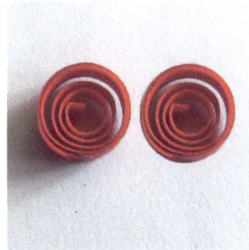

19. Repeat steps 17 and 18 so that you have two loose coils made.

20. Glue one of the coils you have just made to the inside top middle of the bottom wing.

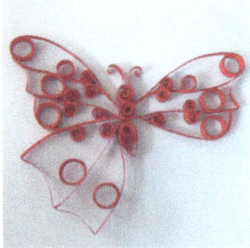

21. Take the second coil and glue it to the inside top of the bottom wing about ¼ inch to the right of the first coil.

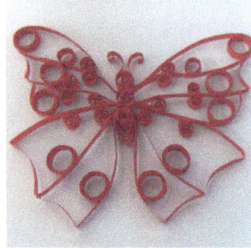

22. Repeat steps 1 to 21 to make the other bottom wing. You are now done your butterfly.

You can make this butterfly in any colour. Play around with the placement of the circles. Add some glitter to the wings if you wish. Use it to decorate cards, or make a bunch of them to hang as a mobile or window hanging.

Simple Dragonfly

Level – Easy

You Will Need:

‣ 1 strip of light green 1/8" (3 mm) quilling paper, 20 inches (50 cm) long
‣ 1 strip of light green 1/8" (3 mm) quilling paper, 16 inches (40 cm) long
‣ 2 strips of light green 1/8" (3 mm) quilling paper, 12 inches (30 cm) long
‣ 1 strip of light green 1/8" (3 mm) quilling paper, 8 inches (20 cm) long
‣ 1 strip of light green 1/8" (3 mm) quilling paper, 4 inches (10 cm) long
‣ 2 strips of light yellow 1/8" (3 mm) quilling paper, 24 inches (60 cm) long
‣ 2 strips of light yellow 1/8" (3 mm) quilling paper, 12 inches (30 cm) long
‣ 2 strips of black 1/8" (3 mm) quilling paper, 8 inches (20 cm) long

Directions:

Making The Body:

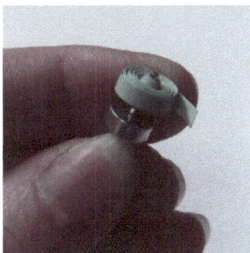

1. Take the 20 inch light green strip and roll it into a tight coil.

2. Glue the end so that it does not unravel.

3. Pinch both ends to make an eye shape.

4. Glue the shape to your card stock with the pointed end up.

23

5. Take the 16 inch light green strip and roll it into a tight coil.

6. Glue down the tail end of the paper so that it does not unravel.

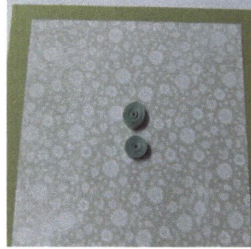

7. Glue the coil down on the card stock just below the first shape , leaving about a ¼ inch space between the two shapes.

8. Take one of the 12 inch light green strips and roll it into a tight coil, gluing the end so that it does not unravel.

9. Repeat step 8 with the second 12 inch light green strip so that you have 2 tight coils the same size.

10. Glue the two coils beneath the ones that are already glued to down. Leave a little space between them and have them positioned slightly to the right of each other.

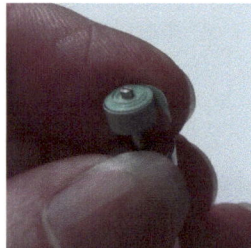

11. Take the 8 inch light green strip and roll it into a tight coil.

12. Glue the end of the coil so that it doesn't unravel.

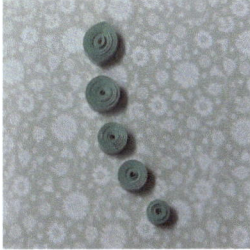

13. Glue the coil to the card stock below and to the right of the previous coils.

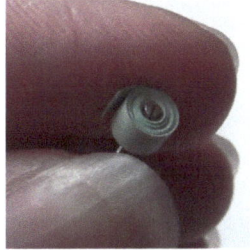

14. Take the 4 inch light green strip and roll it into a tight coil.

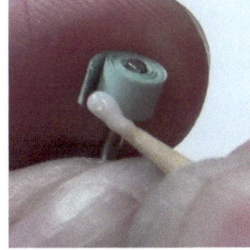

15. Glue the end so that it does not unravel.

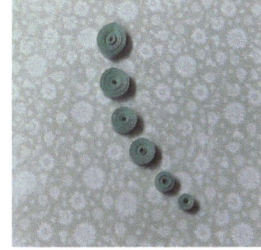

16. Glue this coil to the card stock just below and to the right of the previous ones.

Making The Wings:

1. Take one of the 24 inch light yellow strips and curl it into a loose coil, gluing the end so it doesn't unravel.

2. Pinch one end of the coil so that it makes a tear drop shape. This is a top wing.

3. Repeat steps 1 and 2 so that you have two top wings.

4. Glue one of the top wings to the card stock just to the right of the first body piece.

5. Glue the other top wing to the card stock on the opposite side, just to the left of the first body piece.

6. Take one of the 12 inch light yellow strips and curl it into a loose coil, gluing the end so it doesn't unravel.

7. Pinch one end of the coil so that it makes a tear drop shape. This is a bottom wing.

8. Repeat steps 6 and 7 so that you have two bottom wings.

9. Glue one of the bottom wings to the card stock just to the left of the first body piece and under the top wing.

10. Glue the other bottom wing to the card stock on the opposite side, just to the right of the first body piece and under the top wing.

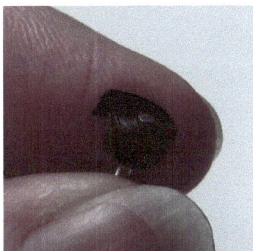

1. Take one of the 8 inch strips of black paper and roll it into a tight coil.

2. Glue the end so that it doesn't unravel. This is an eye.

3. Repeat steps 1 and 2 for the second eye.

4. Glue the eyes onto the card stock just above the first body piece.

OPTIONAL: If you prefer, you can glue all the pieces together. This works better if you wish to make jewelry or a hanging decoration from this design.

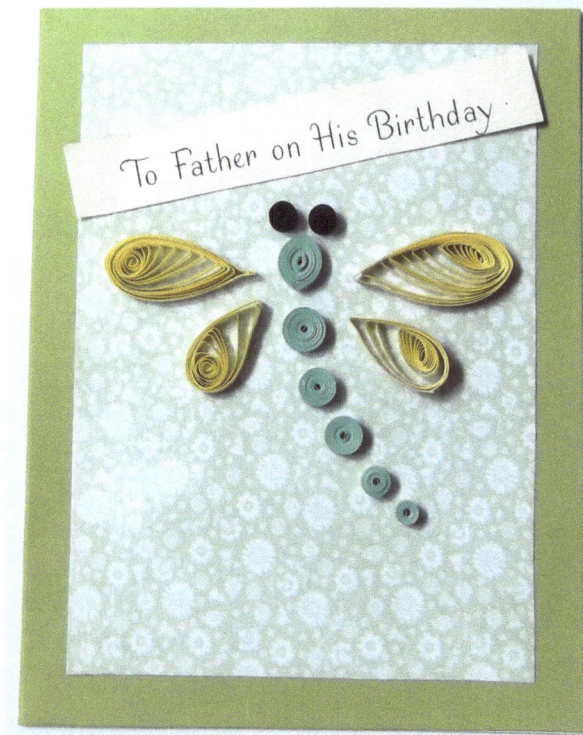

You now have a dragonfly design to embellish your card. Simply add
what ever sentiment you would like and then your card is complete.

Ant

Level – Easy

You Will Need:

‣ 1 strip of dark brown 1/8" (3 mm) quilling paper, 9 inches (23 cm) long
‣ 1 strip of dark brown 1/8" (3 mm) quilling paper, 10 ½ inches (26.5 cm) long
‣ 1 strip of dark brown 1/8" (3 mm) quilling paper, ½ inch (1.5 cm) long
‣ 1 strip of dark brown 1/8" (3 mm) quilling paper, 3 ½ inches (8.5 cm) long

Directions:

Making The Head:

  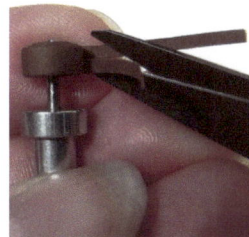 

1. Take the 9 inch dark brown strip and roll it into a tight coil leaving a 1 inch tail.

2. Glue down at the base of the tail so that it does not unravel.

3. Cut length wise up the center of the tail end.

4. Loosely roll the end of one of the split tail pieces into a coil to make an antenna.

5. Roll the other tail piece into a loose coil to make the other antenna.

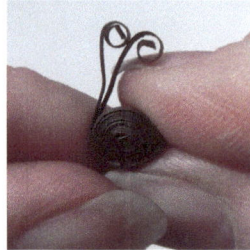

6. Pinch the coil on the side to the right of the antennae so that it gives the ant a pointed face.

7. You now have the ants head made. Set it aside for a moment.

Making The Body:

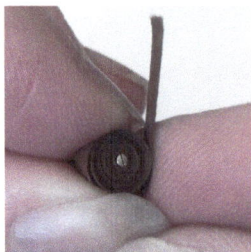

1. Take the 10 ½ inch dark brown strip and roll it into a tight coil leaving a ½ inch long tail.

2. Glue down at the base of the tail so that it does not unravel.

3. With the tail pointing to the right, Squeeze the coil in the middle so that you have an oval shape.

4. Bend the tail end back so that there is a slight curve at the base of it.

5. Cut length wise up the tail of the coil. These are the back legs of the ant.

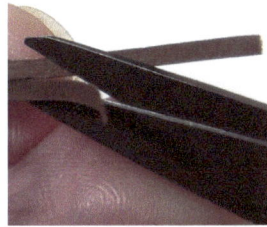

6. Take the ½ inch dark brown piece and cut length wise up the middle. Leave about 1/8 inch uncut. These are the middle legs of the ant.

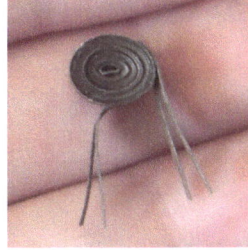

7. With the back legs facing downward, glue the middle legs to the right side of the body.

8. Take the 3 ½ inch dark brown strip and roll it into a tight coil, leaving about ½ inch tail at the end.

9. Glue the coil down by the base of the tail so that it does not unravel.

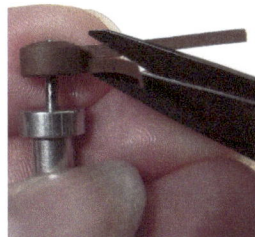

10. Cut lengthwise up the tail of the coil. These are the front legs of the ant.

11. Glue the coil with the front legs to the coil with the back and middle legs.

12. Glue the head onto the body at the top of the front legs.

OPTIONAL: You can make smaller ants by using a 4 inch strip for the head, a 5 inch strip for the body and a 2 ½ inch strip for the middle. The middle leg would only be ¼ inch long and the antennae would only be ½ inch long.

You can make one ant or you can make many and have a whole bunch raiding the picnic basket. What ever you decide, have fun with it!

Bee Hive Trinket Box

Level – Easy

You Will Need:

- 6 strips of yellow 1/16" (1.5 mm) quilling paper, 5 inches (13 cm) long
- 3 strips of black 1/16" (1.5 mm) quilling paper, ¾ inches (2 cm) long
- 3 strips of black 1/16" (1.5 mm) quilling paper, 4 ½ inches (5 cm) long
- 3 strips of black 1/16" (1.5 mm) quilling paper, 1 ¼ inches (3.5 cm) long
- 3 strips of white 1/8" (3mm) quilling paper, ½ inch (1.5 cm) long
- 20 strips of dark brown 1/8" (3mm) quilling paper, 18 inches (45.5 cm) long
- 1 strip of flower patterned paper, 5 inches (13 cm) long and 1 ½ " (4cm) wide
- 22 strips of beige or tan 1/8" (3mm) quilling paper, 17 ½ inches (45 cm) long

Directions:

Making The Bees Bodies:

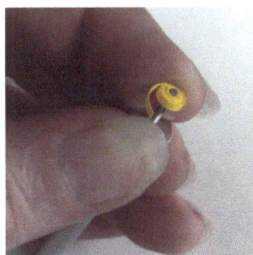

1. Take one of the yellow strips and roll it into a tight coil.

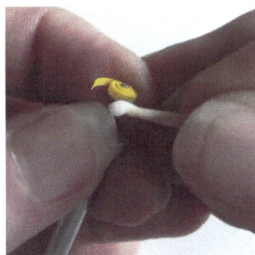

2. Glue the end so that the coil does not unravel.

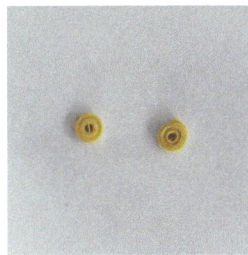

3. Repeat steps 1 and 2 to create a second tight coil.

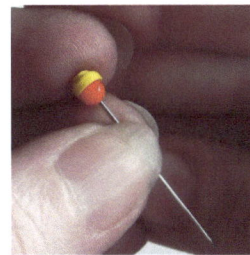

4. Use a round pin head to push up the center of both coils to make two dome shapes.

33

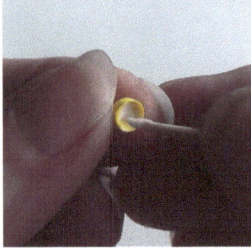

5. Coat the inside of both dome shapes with glue and let them dry.

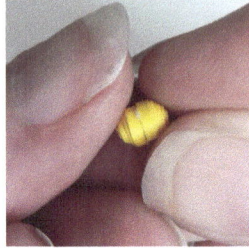

6. Glue both dome shapes together to make an egg shape.

7. Set the egg shape aside to let it dry.

8. Repeat steps 1 to 6 until you have three egg shapes.

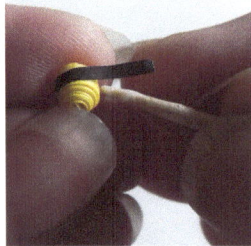

9. Take one of the black ¾ inch long strips and glue it all the way around the center of the yellow egg shape.

10. Repeat step 9 for the other two egg shapes. These are the bee's bodies.

Making The Heads:

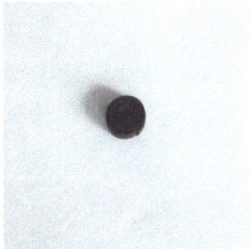

1. Take one of the 4 ½ inch black strips and roll it into a tight coil. Glue the end so that it does not unravel.

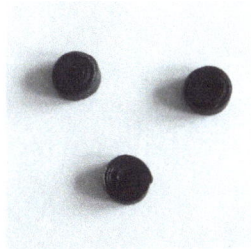

2. Repeat step one for the next 2 strips of 4 ½ inch black paper. You will have 3 tight coils all together.

3. Glue the one of the black coils onto the body of the bee. This is the bee's head.

4. Repeat step 3 for the other two black coils.

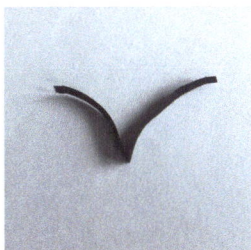

5. Take one of the 1 ¼ inch black strips and fold it in half.

6. Curl both of the folded ends into a loose curl. This is the bee's antennae.

7. Glue the antennae onto the top of the bee's head.

8. Repeat steps 5 to 7 for the other two sets of antennae.

Making The Wings:

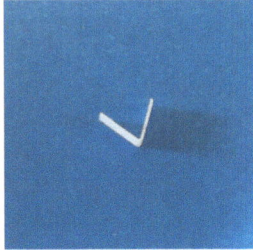

1. Take one of the white strips and fold it in half.

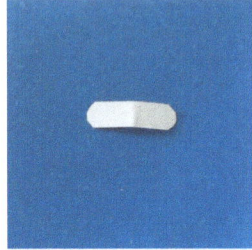

2. With a pair of scissors, round the corners at both ends of the folded white strip. This is the bee's wings.

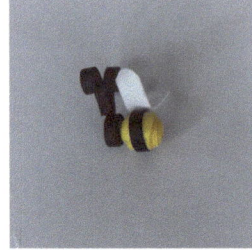

3. Glue the wings onto the back of the bee.

4. Repeat steps 1 to 3 for the wings on the other two bees.

Making The Base:

1. Take the first 18 inch brown strip and roll it into a tight coil. Make sure to glue the end down so that it does not unravel.

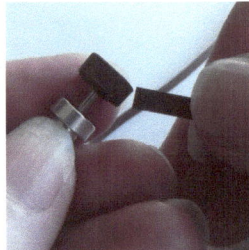

2. Take the next brown strip and glue it to the brown coil where the previous strip left off.

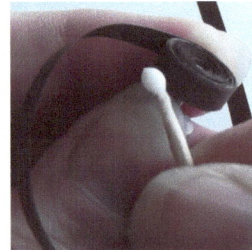

3. Wrap and glue all 20 brown strips around the brown coil, making sure to glue it here and there as you go.

4. When all 20 strips have been wrapped in a coil you will have a circular disc about an inch and a half in diameter.

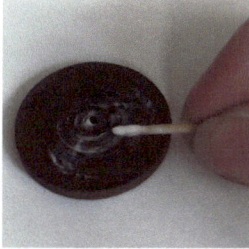

5. *Spread a layer of glue over the entire surface of the brown disc. Then set it aside to dry.*

6. *From a sheet of flower patterned card stock paper, cut a strip that is 5 inches long and 1 ½ inches wide.*

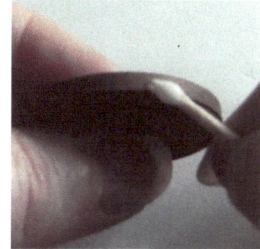

7. *Once the glue on the surface of the disc is dry, add some more glue along the outer edge of the disc.*

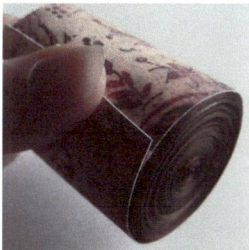

8. *Take the strip of flower patterned paper and glue it around the outer edge of the disc.*

9. *Glue the edge of the flowered paper down to make a small tube.*

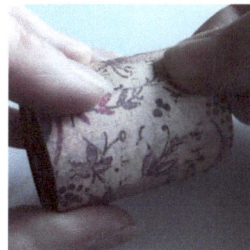

10. *You may have to hold down the egde of the flower patterned paper for a minute or two while the glue dries.*

11. *When it has dried you will have a tube shaped container. Set this aside for now while you work on the bee hive.*

Making The Bee Hive:

1. Take the first 17 ½ inch beige (or tan) strip and roll it into a tight coil. Glue the end down so that it doesn't unravel.

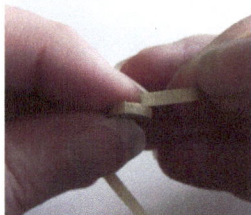

2. Wrap and glue all 22 beige (or tan) strips around the brown coil, making sure to glue it here and there as you go.

3. When all the beige (or tan) strips have been rolled onto the coil you will have a flat disc shape.

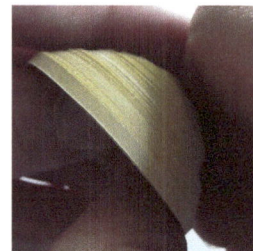

4. Gently push on the center of the disc with your thumbs while supporting the top with your fingers to make a dome shape.

5. The dome does not have to be completely smooth. Some ridges will make the shape look more like a hive.

6. Coat the underside of the dome completely with glue and allow it to dry.

7. Once the underside of the dome is dry, you can glue on the bees.

8. Glue the other bees onto the hive at various points that you think look good.

Place the hive on top of the base and there you have a little bee hive trinket box. You can store your favourite necklace or you can put wrapped candy in them and use them as wedding or party favours.

Bumble Bee

Level – Easy

- 1 strip of yellow 1/8" (3mm) quilling paper, 4 inches (10 cm) long
- 2 strips of black 1/8" (3mm) quilling paper, 4 inches (10 cm) long
- 1 strip of yellow 1/8" (3mm) quilling paper, 6 inches (15 cm) long
- 2 strips of black 1/8" (3mm) quilling paper, 1 inch (3 cm) long
- 1 strip of black 1/8" (3mm) quilling paper, 6 inches (15 cm)
- 1 strip of yellow 1/8" (3mm) quilling paper, 8 inches (20 cm)
- 1 strips of black 1/8" (3mm) quilling paper, 10 inches (25 cm)
- 1 strip of yellow 1/8" (3mm) quilling paper, 10 inches (25 cm)
- 1 strips of black 1/8" (3mm) quilling paper, 8 inches (20 cm)
- 1 strip of yellow 1/8" (3mm) quilling paper, 6 inches (15 cm)
- 1 strips of black 1/8" (3mm) quilling paper, 3 inches (5 cm) long
- 1 strips of black 1/8" (3mm) quilling paper, 2 inches (8 cm) long
- 2 strips of grey 1/8" (3mm) quilling paper, 8 inches (20 cm) long
- 2 strips of grey 1/8" (3mm) quilling paper, 7 inches (18 cm) long

Making The Head:

1. Take the 4 inch yellow strip and roll it into a loose coil. Be sure to glue the end so that it doesn't unravel.

2. Roll one of the 4 inch black strips into a tight coil.

3. Take the other 4 inch black strip and roll it into a tight coil too.

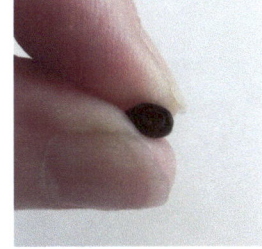

4. Squeeze both of the black coils between your fingers so that they become oval shapes. These are the eyes.

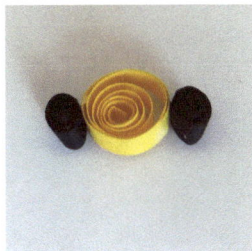

5. Glue both of the eyes onto either side of the yellow coil.

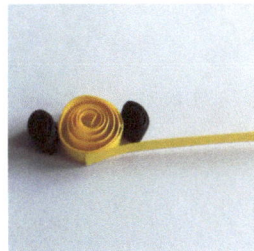

6. Glue the 6 inch yellow strip To the bottom of the yellow coil.

7. Wrap the yellow strip all the way around the face and eyes.

8. Continue to wrap the yellow strip in loose coils around the face until you have come to the end of the strip. Glue the end in place.

9. Take one of the 1 inch black strips and make a loose coil at one end.

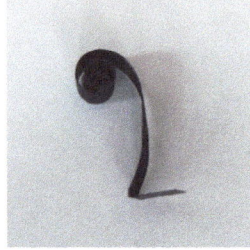

10. Fold a tiny bit of the other end of the black strip so that the coil is in the shape of a fancy looking "2". This is an antenna.

11. Glue the antenna to the top of the bees head.

12. Repeat steps 9 to 11 for the second antenna. You now have the bumble bee's head.

Making The Body:

1. Take the 6 inch black strip and roll it into a loose coil. Make sure to glue down the end.

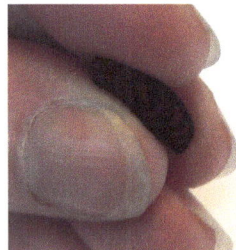

2. Gently squeeze the coil between your fingers.

3. The black coil should be in the shape of a crescent moon.

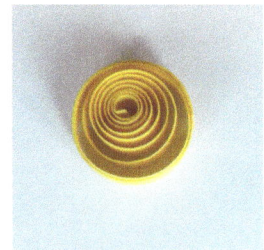

4. Take the 8 inch strip of yellow and roll it into a loose coil and glue the end in place.

5. Gently squeeze the yellow coil between your fingers.

6. Glue the black crescent moon shape on top of the yellow shape.

7. Roll the 10 inch black strip into a loose coil and glue the end in place.

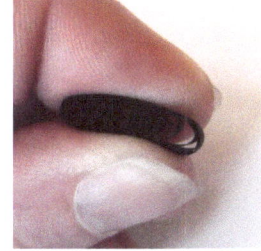

8. Gently squeeze the black coil between your fingers.

9. Glue the squished black coil onto the bottom of the yellow shape.

10. Roll the 10 inch yellow strip into a loose coil and glue the end in place.

11. Gently squeeze the yellow coil between your fingers top make a crescent shape.

12. Glue the yellow crescent shape to the bottom of the previous black crescent shape.

13. Roll the 8 inch black strip into a loose coil and glue the end in place so that it doesn't unravel.

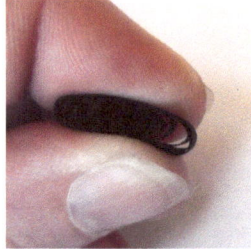

14. Gently squeeze the black coil between your fingers to make another crescent shape.

15. Glue the new black crescent shape to the bottom of the previous yellow crescent shape.

16. Roll the 6 inch yellow strip into a loose coil and glue the end in place so that it does not unravel.

17. Gently squeeze the yellow coil between your fingers to make another crescent shape.

18. Glue the final yellow crescent onto the bottom of the previous black crescent shape.

19. Glue the 3 inch black strip to the bottom edge of the yellow crescent shape.

20. Wrap the black strip all the way around the outside of the body, pulling the crescents fairly tight together. Be sure to glue the end in place.

21. Take the 2 inch black strip and roll it into a tight coil. Glue the end so that it does nto unravel.

22. Squish the black coil into a triangle shape. This is the stinger.

23. Glue the stinger onto the bottom of the body.

24. Glue the head onto the body.

Making The Wings:

1. Take one of the 8 inch grey strips and roll one end into a loose coil.

2. Make a fold in the grey strip about 1 and ½ inches up the tail end so that it makes a tear drop shape.

3. Glue the tail end to the side of the coiled end.

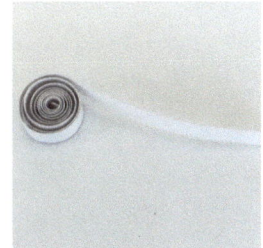

4. Take one of the 7 inch grey strips and roll one end into a loose coil.

5. Make a fold in the grey strip about 1 and ¼ inches up the tail end so that it makes a tear drop shape.

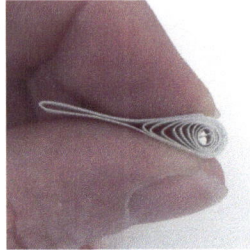

6. Pinch the middle of the tear drop shape between your fingers.

7. Glue the tail end to the outside edge of the coil.

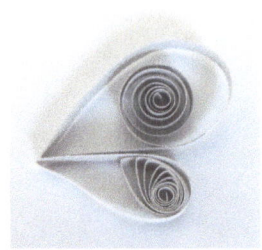

8. Glue the first tear drop shape to the side of the second smaller tear drop shape.

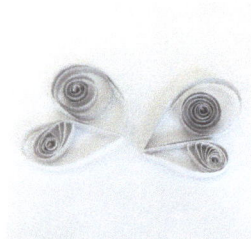

9. Repeat steps 1 to 8 so that you have a second set of wings.

10. Glue both sets of wings onto both sides of the body.

You now have a bumble bee to decorate your project with. You can make Valentine's Day cards, birthday cards, and more using this little bee. Or make more and hang them from string to make a mobile to hang in the window.

Lady Bug

Level – Easy

- 2 strips of black 1/8" (3mm) quilling paper, 2 inches (5 cm) long
- 2 strips of red 1/8" (3mm) quilling paper, 6 inches (15 cm) long
- 2 strips of black 1/8" (3mm) quilling paper, 1 ½ inches (4 cm) long
- 2 strips of black 1/8" (3mm) quilling paper, 6 inch (15 cm) long

Making The Wings:

1. Roll one of the 2 inch black strips into a tight coil. Be sure to glue down the end so that it doesn't unravel.

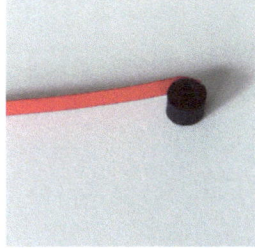

2. Take one of the red strips and glue one end to the side of the black coil.

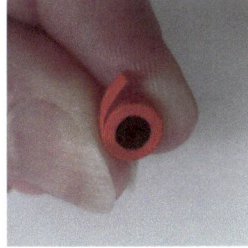

3. Roll the red strip all the way around the black coil.

4. Let go of the red strip so that it becomes a loose coil. Then glue the tail end down so that it does not unravel any further.

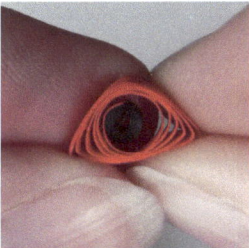

5. Pinch both ends of the red coil to make a half moon shape.

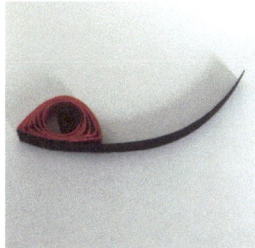

6. Take one of the 1 ½ inch black strips and glue it to the flat side of the half moon shape.

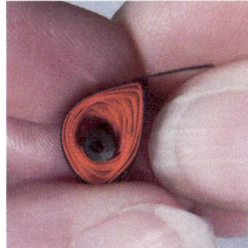

7. Wrap the black strip all the way around the half moon shape.

8. Glue the end of the black strip in place. You now have a lady bug wing.

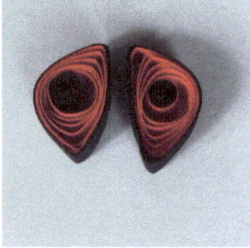

9. Repeat steps 1 to 8 so that you have two lady bug wings.

10. Glue the flat ends of both wings together. Set these aside for now.

Making The Head:

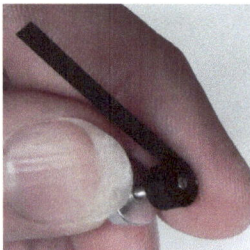

1. Take one of the 6 inch black strips and roll it into a tight coil, leaving a 1 inch tail.

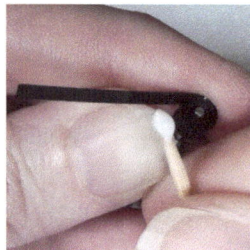

2. Glue the black strip near the base of the tail so that it does not unravel.

3. Make a loose curl in the tail end of the black strip. This is an eye and antenna.

4. Repeat steps 1 to 3 so that you have two eyes and two antennae.

5. Glue the eyes and antennae together.

6. Glue the eyes and antennae to the wings.

You now have a little lady bug! These cute little bugs are great for decorating greeting cards, as gift tags or as name place cards. They would look very nice on tables for weddings or parties.

Firefly

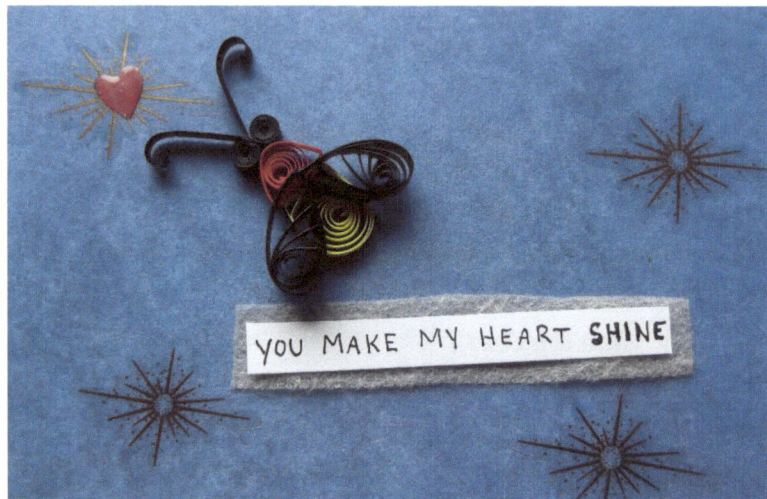

YOU MAKE MY HEART SHINE

Level – Easy

You Will Need:

▸ 1 strip of yellow 1/8" (3mm) quilling paper, 7 inches (18 cm) long
▸ 1 strip of red 1/8" (3mm) quilling paper, 5 inches (13 cm) long
▸ 2 strips of black 1/8" (3mm) quilling paper, 8 inches (20.5 cm) long
▸ 2 strips of black 1/8" (3mm) quilling paper, 5 inch (13 cm) long

Directions:

Making The Body:

1. Roll and glue the yellow strip into a loose coil.

2. Pinch the coil to make it flat at one end.

3. Roll and glue the red strip into a loose coil.

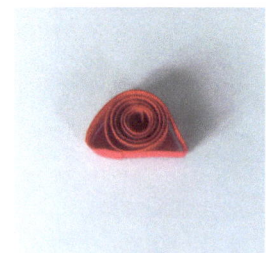

4. Pinch the red coil into a half moon shape.

5. Glue the flat part of the red shape to the flat part of the yellow shape. This is the body.

6. Roll and glue one of the 8 inch black strips into a loose coil.

7. Pinch one end of the black coil to make a tear drop shape. This is a wing.

8. Repeat steps 6 and 7 to create a second wing.

9. Glue one wing on top and to the right of the body.

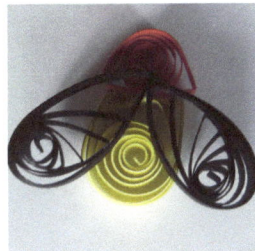

10. Glue the second wing on the body beside the first one.

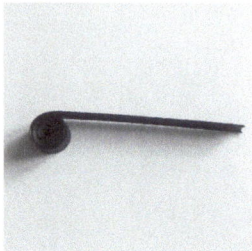

1. Take one of the 5 inch black strips and roll and glue it into a tight coil leaving a tail about one inch long.

2. Make a little bit of a curl at the end of the tail. This is an eye and antennae.

3. Repeat steps 1 and 2 to create a second set of eyes and antennae. Glue the two eyes and antennae together.

4. Glue the eyes and antennae to the red part of the body.

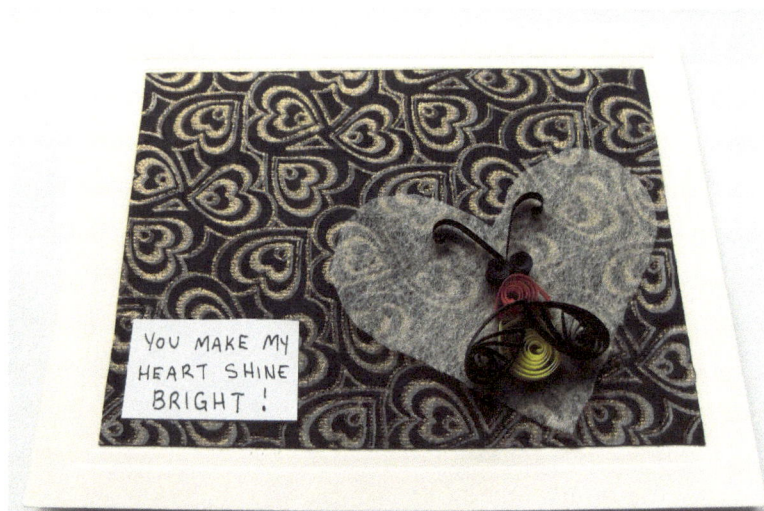

Let this little firefly light up your projects!

Spider

Level – Easy

You Will Need:

- 1 strip of brown 1/8" (3mm) quilling paper, 17 inches (43 cm) long
- 2 strips of yellow 1/16" (1.5 mm) quilling paper, 3 inches (8 cm) long
- 8 strips of brown 1/16" (1.5 mm) quilling paper, 1 inch (2.5 cm) long

Directions:

Making The Body:

 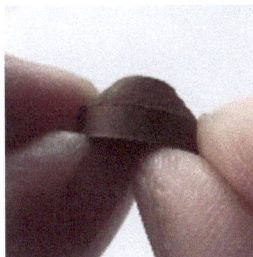 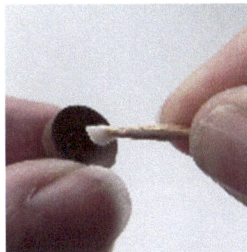 

1. *Roll and glue the 17 inch brown strip into a tight solid coil.*

2. *Push the center of the brown coil out until it forms a dome.*

3. *Coat the inner side of the dome with glue so that it won't fall apart.*

4. *This is the spider's body. Set it aside and let it dry.*

Making The Eyes:

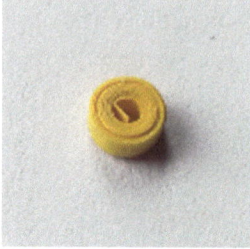

1. Roll one of the yellow strips into a tight coil.

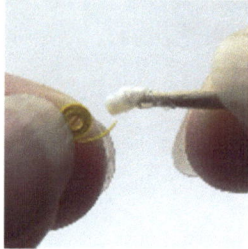

2. Glue the end so that the coil does not unravel.

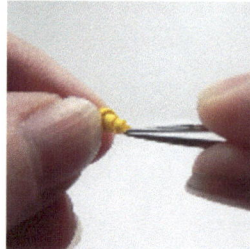

3. Take a pair of tweezers and pull the middle of the coil out from the center a little bit.

4. Cut off the yellow piece that you have pulled from the center.

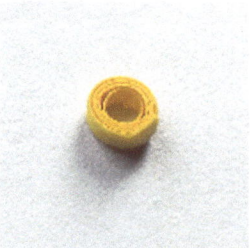

5. You should now have a circle with an open center. This is an eye.

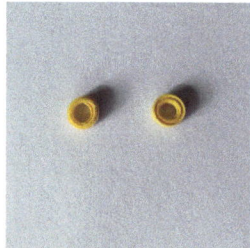

6. Repeat steps 1 to 5 to make a second eye.

7. Glue both of the eyes onto the spider's body.

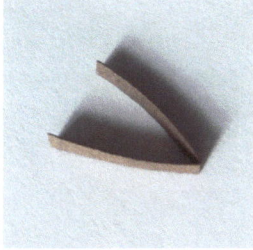

1. Take one of the 1 inch brown strips and fold it in half to make a "V" shape.

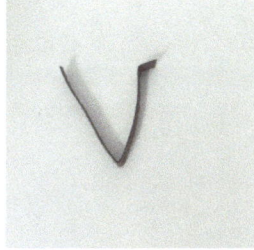

2. Fold one end of the "V" over about ¼ inch to make a foot.

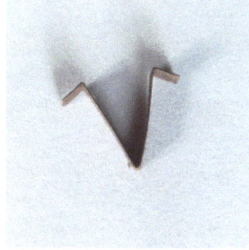

3. Fold the other end of the "V" over to make a place to attach the leg to the body.

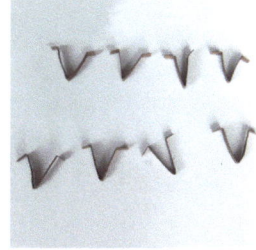

4. Repeat steps 1 to 3 for the other seven strips. You now have 8 spider legs.

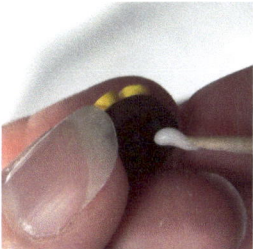

5. Add some glue to one side of the under side of the body .

6. Attach 4 legs to the under side of the spider's body.

7. Add some glue to the other side underneath the spider's body.

8. Attach the remaining 4 legs to the underside of the body.

Now you are ready to add your spider to your Halloween decorations. Hang him by a thread or have him sit near the candy bowl.

House Fly

Level – Easy

You Will Need:

- 2 strips of grey 1/8" (3mm) quilling paper, 10 inches (25 cm) long
- 1 strip of white 1/16" (1.5 mm) quilling paper, 2 inches (5 cm) long
- 1 strip of black 1/16" (1.5mm) quilling paper, 2 ½ inches (6.5 cm) long
- 3 strips of black 1/8" (3mm) quilling paper, 1 inch (2.5 cm) long
- 1 strip of white 1/4" (7mm) quilling paper, ¾ inches (2 cm) long

Directions:

Making The Body and Eyes:

 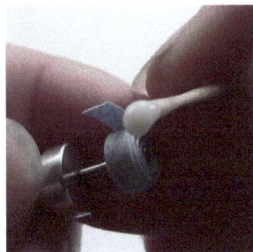 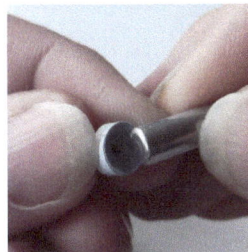 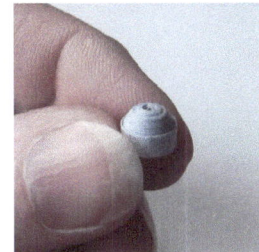

1. Take one of the 10 inch grey strips and roll it into a tight coil.

2. Glue the end down so that it does not unravel.

3. Using the end of a pencil or quilling tool, push the inside up.

4. You should now have a dome shape.

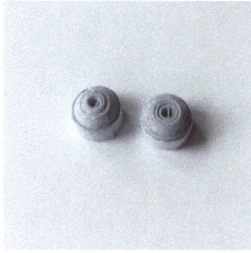

5. *Repeat steps 1 to 4 so that you have two dome shapes.*

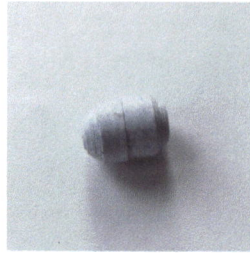

6. *Glue the two dome shapes together to form one pill shape. This is the body.*

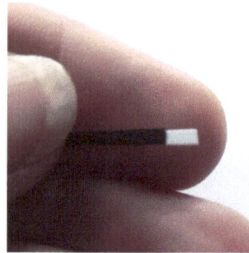

7. *Take the 2 ½ inch long black strip and glue the end of it about a ¼ inch down from the end of the white strip.*

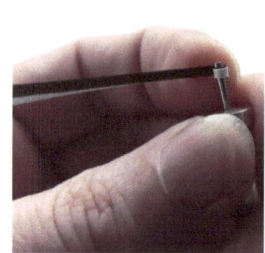

8. *Roll both strips together into one tight coil.*

9. *Glue the end down. so that the coil does not unravel. You now have one fly eye.*

10. *Repeat steps 7 to 9 to make a second eye.*

11. *Glue one of the eyes to one end of the body.*

12. *Glue the other eye beside the first one. Both of the eyes should be on an angle.*

1. Take two of the black 1 inch strips and glue them together to form an "X".

2. Take the third black 1 inch strip and glue it across the "X" shape. These are the legs.

3. Fold the ends of each of the legs up to make little feet.

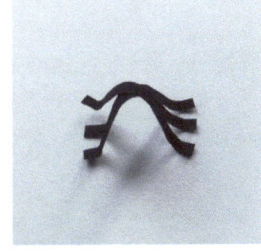

4. Bend the legs into a "U" shape so that all of the feet are touching the ground.

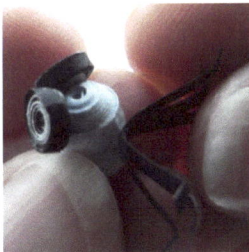

5. Glue the legs to the under side of the body.

6. Take the ¾ inch white strip of paper and fold it in half to make a "V" shape.

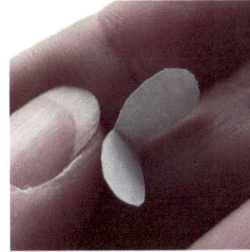

7. Cut the corners of the "V" shape to make them round. These will be your wings.

8. Glue the wings onto the back of the body.

You now have a little fly. Make more little fly friends and use them to decorate paper weights. They would also be a hit for Halloween parties or kids birthday parties.

Filigree Dragonfly

Level – Easy

- 1 strip of bright blue 1/8" (3mm) quilling paper, 6 inches (15 cm) long
- 2 strips of bright blue 1/8" (3mm) quilling paper, 2 ½ inches (6.5 cm) long
- 2 strips of bright blue 1/8" (3mm) quilling paper, 2 inches (5 cm) long
- 1 strips of turqoise 1/8" (3mm) quilling paper, 3 ½ inches (8 cm) long
- 2 strips of turqoise 1/8" (3mm) quilling paper, 4 inches (10 cm) long
- 3 strips of turqoise 1/8" (3mm) quilling paper, 3 inches (8 cm) long
- 1 strips of mint green 1/8" (3mm) quilling paper, ¾ inch (2 cm) long
- 1 strips of mint green 1/8" (3mm) quilling paper, 9 inches (8 cm) long
- 1 strips of mint green 1/8" (3mm) quilling paper, 12 inches (8 cm) long
- 2 strips of black 1/8" (3mm) quilling paper, 4 inches (10 cm) long

Making The Wings:

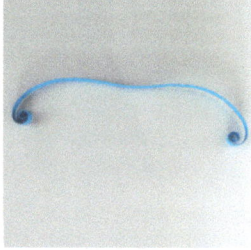

1. Take the 6 inch bright blue strip and curl both ends towards each other.

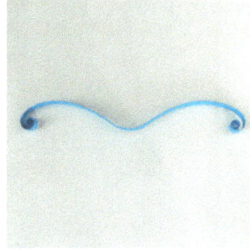

2. In the very center of the 6 inch strip create a slight upward curve.

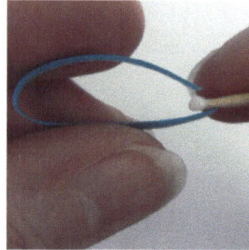

3. Take the 2 ½ inch bright blue strips and glue them both into tear drop shapes.

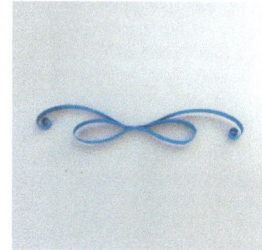

4. Glue the tear drop shapes on the under side of the 6 inch strip, one on each side of the upward curve .

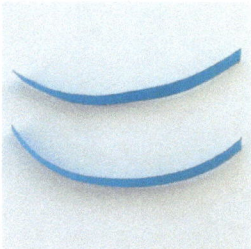

5. Take both of the 2 inch bright blue strips and give them a gentle curve so that they look like little smiles.

6. Glue the curved strips to the under side of the tear drop shapes and to the curls of the 6 inch strips. These are the bottom wings.

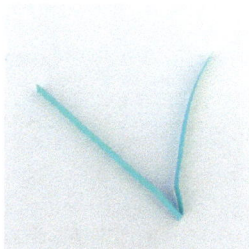

7. Take the 3 ½ inch turquoise strip and fold it in half.

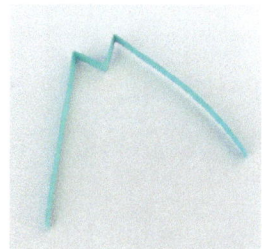

8. About ½ inch up both sides, fold both ends back towards the middle, creating an "M" shape.

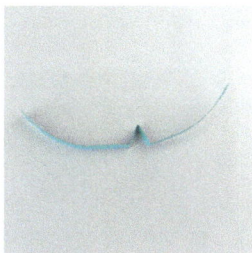

9. Flip the "M" upside down and curve both of the tail ends slightly towards the center.

10. Glue the bottom of the upside down "M" to the top of the wings.

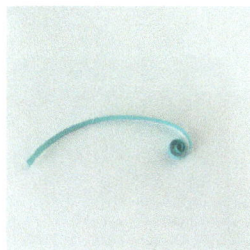

11. Take one of the 4 inch turquoise strips and curl one end into a loose coil. Give the tail end a little bit of a curve too.

12. Glue the tail end to inner corner of the upside down "M" shape and the curled end to the curled end of the wing.

13. Repeat steps 11 and 12 for the other 4 inch turquoise strip on the opposite side. These are the top wings.

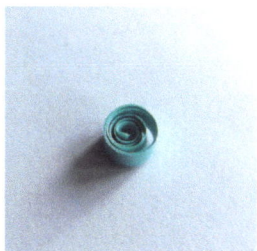

14. Take one of the 3 inch turquoise strips and roll it into a loose coil, making sure to glue down the end so that it does not unravel.

15. Glue the turquoise coil into the curve of the tear drop shape on the bottom wing.

16. Repeat steps 14 and 15 for another 3 inch turquoise strip. You now have a full set of wings for your dragonfly.

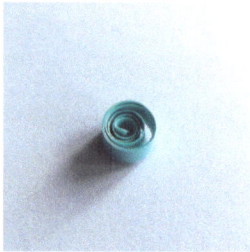

1. Take the last 3 inch turquoise strip and roll it into a loose coil, being sure to glue down the tail end so that it doesn't unravel.

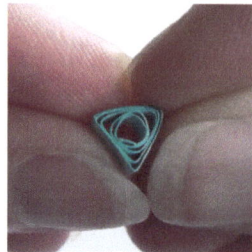

2. Take the turquoise coil and pinch it between your fingers to create a triangle shape.

3. Glue the triangle shape to the under side of the wings in the center just below the point of the upside down "M" .

4. Take the ¾ inch mint green strip and fold it in half to make a "V" shape.

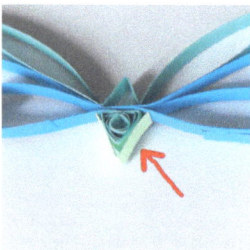

5. Glue the mint green "V" shape to the outer edge of the triangle shape that is attached to the underside of the wings.

6. Take the 9 inch mint green strip and roll it into a loose coil. Be sure to glue down the end so that it does not unravel.

7. Pinch both ends of the mint green coil to make an "eye" shape.

8. Glue one of the pointed ends of the "eye shape" and attach it to the pointed end of the triangle that is on the bottom wings.

9. Take the 12 inch mint green strip and roll it into a loose coil. Be sure to glue down the end so that it doesn't unravel.

10. Pinch one end of the coil so that you have a tear drop shape.

11. Glue the tip of the tear drop shape to the tip of the eye shape.

Making The Eyes:

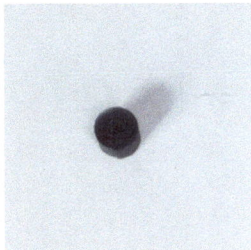

1. Roll one of the 4 inch black strips into a tight coil.

2. Roll the second 4 inch black strip into a tight coil and glue it to the side of the first black coil. These are the eyes.

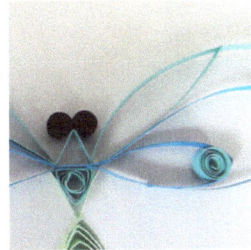

3. Glue the eyes to the point at the top of the wings.

You now have a filigree dragonfly. This makes a beautiful window hanging or a great Mother's Day card.

Damsel Fly

Level – Intermediate

You Will Need:

- 1 strip of green 1/8" (3mm) quilling paper, 5 inches (13 cm) long
- 4 strips of green 1/8" (3mm) quilling paper, 6 inches (15.5 cm) long
- 2 strips of black 1/8" (3mm) quilling paper, 4 inches (10 cm) long
- 4 strips of black 1/16" (1.5 mm) quilling paper, 5 ¾ inches (14.5 cm) long
- 4 strips of irridescent ribbon or paper 1 ½ inches (4 cm) long
- 2 green rhinestones

Directions:

Making The Body:

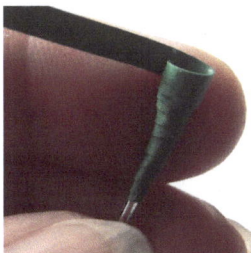

1. Take the 5 inch green strip and roll it into a cone shape.

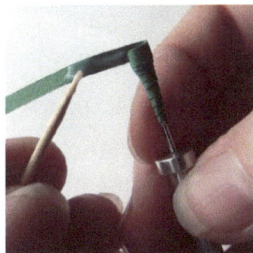

2. Be sure to glue the strip as you go so that the cone holds its shape.

3 Take one of the 6 inch green strips and roll it into a tight coil.

4. Also make tight coils out of the other three 6 inch green strips.

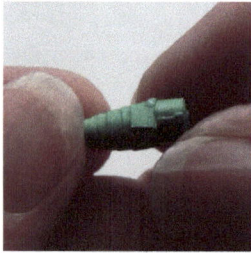

5. Glue one of the tight coils onto the open end of the cone shape.

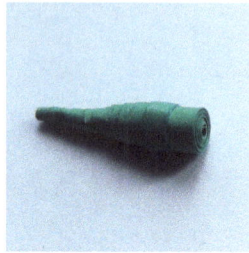

6. Glue another green coil onto the previous one.

7. Continue to glue the green coils onto each other until all the green coils are glued together. This is the body.

Making The Eyes:

1. Take the black 4 inch strip and roll it into a tight coil. Make sure to glue the end down so that it does not unravel.

2. Repeat for the second 4 inch black strip. These are the eyes.

3. Glue the eyes, side by side, onto the widest end of the body.

Making The Wings:

1. With one of the 5 ¾ inch strips of black, begin to wrap it around the first prong of the quilling comb.

2. Continue to wrap up and down, alternating between the high and low numbers until you reach the center.

**Note: If you do not have a quilling comb, try using a hair comb. Or, just make a loose coil and pinch the middle to make a cigar shape.

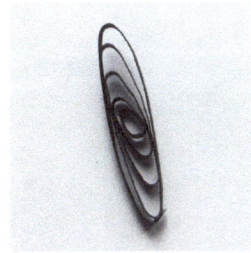

3. Slide the wrapped strip off of the prongs and glue the ends down so it doesn't unravel.

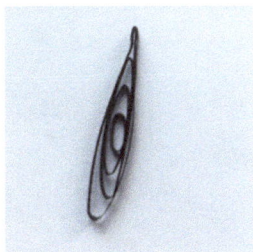

4. Pinch one end so that you have an elongated tear drop shape.

5. Repeat steps 1 to 4 for the other three 5 ¾ inch black strips. These are the wings.

6. Glue the wings onto the pieces of irridescent paper or ribbon and let them dry.

7. When the glue has dried cut around the edges and trim off the excess irridescent paper.

8. Glue two of the wings together, side by side.

9. Glue the other two wings together, side by side. You now have two sets of wings.

10. Glue one set of wings to the top of the body.

11. Then glue the second set of wings to the top of the body.

12. Glue some green rhinestones onto the black eyes.

13. If you wish you can glue a pin to the underside of the damsel fly to make it into a brooch.

Once your damsel fly is complete you can show it off by wearing it or by decorating gifts with it. Whatever you decide, it is sure to be a hit with your friends and family.

Cricket

Level – Intermediate

You Will Need:

- 1 strip of beige 1/8" (3mm) quilling paper, 9 ½ inches (24 cm) long
- 1 strip of beige 1/8" (3mm) quilling paper, 5 inches (12.5 cm) long
- 1 strip of beige 1/8" (3mm) quilling paper, 10 inches (25 cm) long
- 2 strips of beige 1/8" (3mm) quilling paper, ½ inch (1.5 cm) long
- 2 strips of dark brown 1/8" (3mm) quilling paper, 1 ¼ inch (3.5 cm) long
- 4 strips of dark brown 1/16" (1.5 mm) quilling paper, ½ inch (1.5 cm) long
- 2 strips of mottled brown paper 5/8 inches (1.5 cm) long x ¼ inch wide (7mm)

Directions:

Making The Head:

1. Roll the 9 ½ inch beige strip into a tight coil. Glue the end but leave a ½ inch tail.

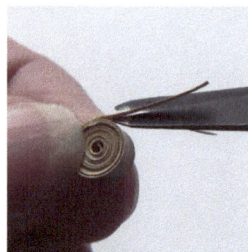

2. Make a cut length wise down the middle of the tail piece.

3. Curl the two tail pieces to make the antennae.

4. You now have the head of a cricket.

Making The Body:

1. Take the 5 inch beige strip and roll it into a cone shape.

2. Be sure to glue the strip as you roll the cone so that it doesn't lose shape.

3. Once the cone is rolled, snip a small part of the tip off so that it isn't so pointy.

4. Glue the head onto the end of the cone that you just snipped off.

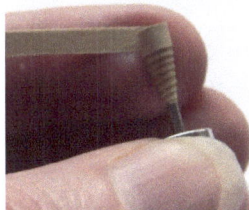

5. Take the 10 inch beige strip and also roll it into a cone shape.

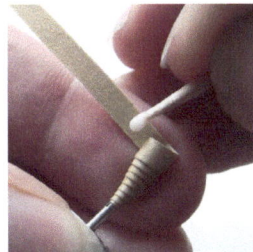

6. It is important to glue as you roll so that it doesn't unravel.

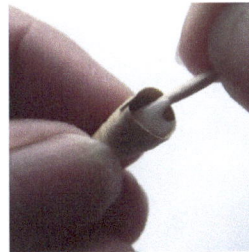

7. Add some glue to the inside edges of the cone.

8. Glue the cone with the head attached to it to the inside of the larger cone.

9. Take one of the ½ inch beige strips and glue it diagonally from the top of the cricket's back, under it's head, and to the bottom of it's body.

10. Repeat step 9 for the second 1/2 inch beige strip for the opposite side. The two strips should criss cross each other under the head.

Making The Legs:

1. Take the 1 ¼ inch dark brown strip and cut it length wise. Leave a bit of the end uncut so that it looks like a foot.

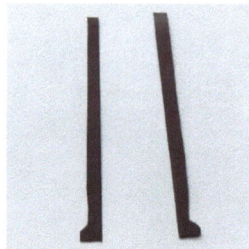

2. Repeat with the second 1 ¼ inch dark brown strip, but cut it in the opposite direction. You now have two hind legs.

3. Glue one of the hind legs to the back of the body so that it sticks straight out and the foot is facing toward the head.

4. Glue the other hind leg to the back on the opposite side.

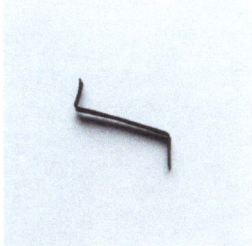

5. Take one of the ½ inch dark brown strips and fold down a bit of the ends going in oppsosite directions from each other. It should look like a "Z" shape.

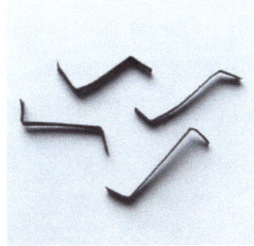

6. Repeat the process for the rest of the ½ inch dark brown strips. You now have four front legs.

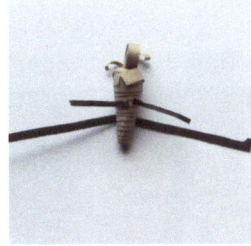

7. Glue two of the front legs to the middle of the belly

8. Glue the other two front legs to the front part of the belly. Have them angle out towards the head.

Making The Wings:

1. Cut 2 strips of mottled brown paper about 5/8 inches long by ¼ inch wide.

2. Cut both of the mottled brown strips into tear drop shapes. These are the wings.

3. Glue the wings onto the back of the cricket.

1. Fold both of the back legs up towards the back of the cricket just a little past where they come out from under the wings.

2. Make another fold in both of the hind legs about a ½ inch from the foot.

3. Fold both of the back feet into an upward position.

4. The cricket should sit back on his hind legs with his front legs supporting his body. You may have to adjust the positioning of the legs a little to get him to sit the way you would like him to sit.

Your cricket is complete! He would look lovely sitting among your plants and flowers.

Shad Fly

Level – Intermediate

You Will Need:

- 1 strip of dark brown 1/8" (3 mm) quilling paper, 8 inches (20 cm) long
- 2 strips of dark brown 1/8" (3 mm) quilling paper, 9 inches (23 cm) long
- 2 strips of dark brown 1/16" (1.5 mm) quilling paper, 1 inch (2.5 cm) long
- 1 strips of dark brown 1/8" (3 mm) quilling paper, 8 inches (20 cm) long
- 2 strips of black 1/8" (3 mm) quilling paper, 1 ½ inch (4 cm) long
- 2 strips of beige 1/8" (3 mm) quilling paper, 2 ½ inch (6.5 cm) long
- 2 strips of black 1/16" (1.5 mm) quilling paper, 1 ¼ inches (3.5 cm) long
- 2 strips of black 1/16" (1.5 mm) quilling paper, 1 inch (2.5 cm) long
- 1 sheet of silver or grey tissue paper
- 2 strips of grey 1/16" (1.5 mm) quilling paper, 3 inches (8 cm) long
- 2 strips of grey 1/16" (1.5 mm) quilling paper, 3 inches (8 cm) long
- 2 strips of grey 1/16" (1.5 mm) quilling paper, 12 inches (30 cm) long

Making The Body:

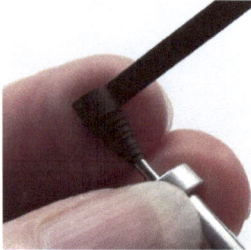

1. Take the 8 inch dark brown strip and roll it into a cone shape.

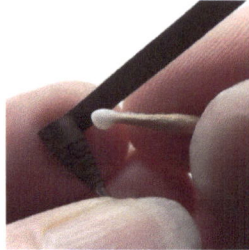

2. You will need to be sure to glue the entire strip as you roll the cone shape so that it will maintain it's shape.

3. Once the cone is made, bend the pointed end up in the air just a little bit so that the cone is slightly curved.

4. Take one of the 9 inch dark brown strips and roll it into a tight coil. Be sure to glue down the end so that it doesn't unravel.

5. Repeat step 4 to make a second tight coil out of the other 9 inch dark brown strip.

6. Glue both of the tight coils, one on top of the other, to the wide open end of the cone shape.

7. Take the two 1 inch dark brown strips and cut them on an angle at both ends to make the ends pointed.

8. Glue the two pointed pieces together in a narrow "V" shape.

9. Gently curve the "V" shape upwards.

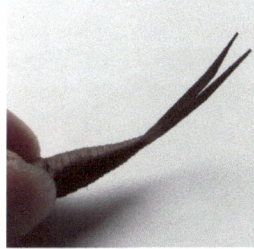

10. Glue the end of the "V" shape into the small hole at the pointed end of the cone shape. (If there is no hole you may have to cut one, but do not make it very big). This is the body.

11. Take an 8 inch dark brown strip and roll it into a tight coil. Be sure to glue the end down so that it doesn't unravel. This is the head.

12. Glue the side of the head to the flat, wide end of the body.

Making The Eyes:

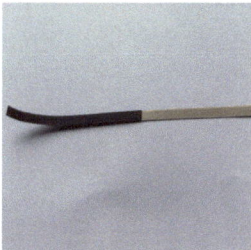

1. Glue the end of the 1 ½ inch black strip to the end of the 2 ½ inch beige strip to make one long strip.

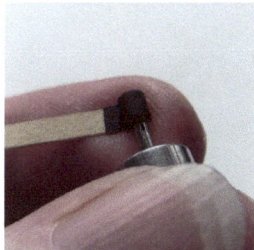

2. Roll this new long strip into a tight coil starting from the black end. Glue it so that it does not unravel.

3. Repeat steps 1 and 2 so that you now have two eyes.

4. Glue the eyes to the head. This can sometimes be a bit tricky because of the angles they should be on.

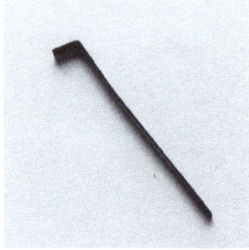

1. Take one of the 1 ¼ inch black strips and fold the end over at about the ¼ inch mark.

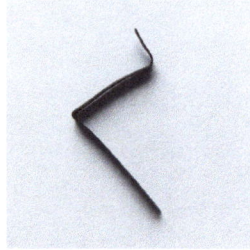

2. Make another fold in the opposite direction about half way up the strip.

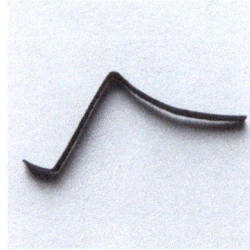

3. Make a gentle curve in the longer end of the strip.

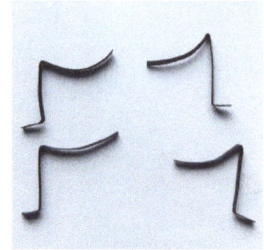

4. Repeat steps 1 to 3 for the other 1 ¼ inch black strips so that you have four back legs.

5. Glue one of the back legs to the underside of the body. Position it somewhere near the head but not too close to it.

6. Glue the rest of the back legs on close to where you glued the first one. Two legs on each side of the body.

7. The four legs will balance your shad fly when he is sitting on his belly. You can adjust them if they aren't sitting quite right.

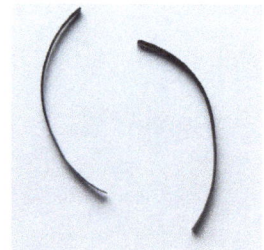

8. Take the two 1 ¼ black strips and put a gentle curve into both of them.

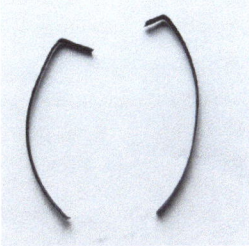

9. Fold about ¼ inch of the end of both the curved strips. These are the front legs.

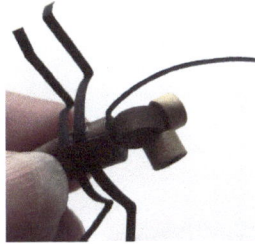

10. Glue the folded part of one of the front legs to the end of the body located just behind the head.

11. Repeat for the second front leg on the opposite side of the head.

Making The Wings:

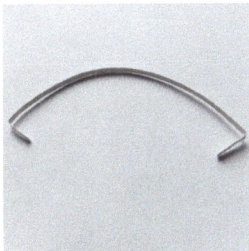

1. Take one of the 3 inch grey strips and fold both ends over about ½ inch. Then make a gentle curve in the middle.

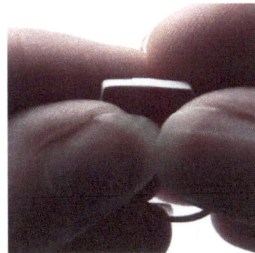

2. Glue the two folded ends together.

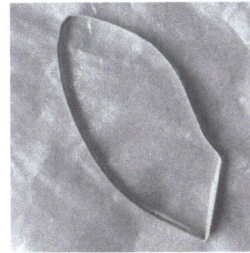

3. Shape the curved end into any sort of wing shape you'd like. Then glue this to a piece of grey or silver tissue paper.

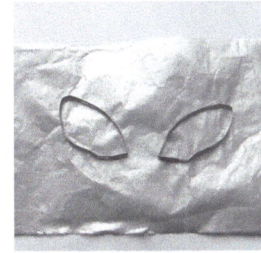

4. Repeat steps 1 to 3 for the other 3 inch grey strip.

5. Take the 12 inch grey strip and roll it into a loose coil. Glue the end so that it doesn't unravel and lose shape.

6. Coat one side of the coil with glue. The inner coils may move around somewhat but that's OK.

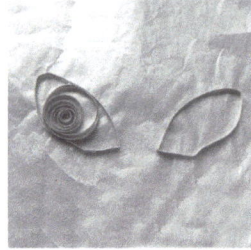

7. Take the coil coated in glue and place it, glue side down, into the center of the wing that is glued to the tissue paper.

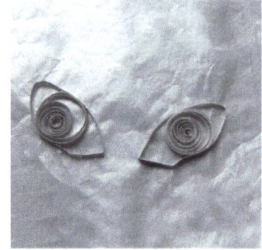

8. Repeat steps 5 to 7 for the other 12 inch grey strip. Then let the glue dry for a few minutes. These are the wings.

9. Once the glue is dry, cut the excess tissue paper off of the wings.

10. You now have two silvery wings for your shadfly.

11. Glue the flat end of one wing to the middle of the body between the four legs.

12. Glue the other wing beside the first one. The two flat sides should be facing each other, and the raised sides with the coils should be facing out.

Every year in the city of North Bay, Ontario, around the month of June, thousands of these little guys are attracted to the lights and come up from the lakes to hang out on the city's buildings, streets and lamp posts. They do nothing much but just sit there. So I am sure your paper version will be happy to sit just about anywhere you would like to put him as well.

ABOUT THE AUTHOR

Dana Woodard was born and raised in North Bay, Ontario, Canada. She was first introduced to quilling when she was a teenager by her mother who showed her how to make some beautiful snowflake Christmas decorations. She only just dabbled in quilling and over the years she set it aside and forgot about it.

Then she met Moira Hiscock who re-introduced the craft to her and once again she was hooked. Together with Moira she created her first book called "Pond Life : Paper Quilling Projects" and published it.

As the designs were thought up and filled the pages, she realized that she had more designs than expected and so this book became her next project. Finding ideas and designs to fill this book may have been easy but finding a name for this book was more challenging. So a big thank you goes out to Judy Brophey who helped her name this book.

Like most crafters, Dana is interested in more than one craft. She also enjoys Iris folding, needle felting, card making, polymer clay, drawing and sewing. She is never bored because she always has some craft or other on the go or is learning something new.

She looks forward to creating the next book for you. You can read more about Dana Woodard and other books that she has published by following her author profile on Good Reads at: www.goodreads.com